SRA Reading Mastery

Signature Edition

Language
Workbook C & D

Siegfried Engelmann
Jean Osborn

 **SRA**

Columbus, OH

Lesson 86

Name _____

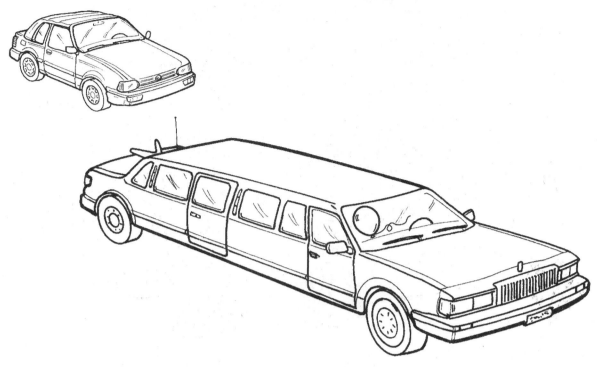

"What is in the big car?" "What did you draw in the small car?" "What color are they?"

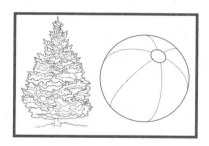 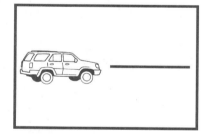

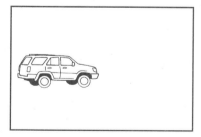  

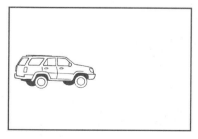  

"Touch a box you circled." "What's in the box?" "What did you draw?" "Touch another box you circled."
"What's in the box?" "What did you draw?"

Side 1 _____

Lesson 86   Name _____

"Show me the monkey that is big." "Show me the monkey that is small."

Point to a circle. "What is this?" "What color is it?" Point to a rectangle. "What is this?" "What color is it?"

Side 2 _____

Lesson 87   Name _____

"What is in front of the old woman?" "What did you draw in front of the young woman?" "What color are they?"

"Touch some food." "Touch a vehicle." "Touch another food." "Touch another vehicle."

Side 1 _____

Lesson 87   Name _____

"Show me a black animal." "Where does it go?" "Show me a white animal." "Where does it go?"

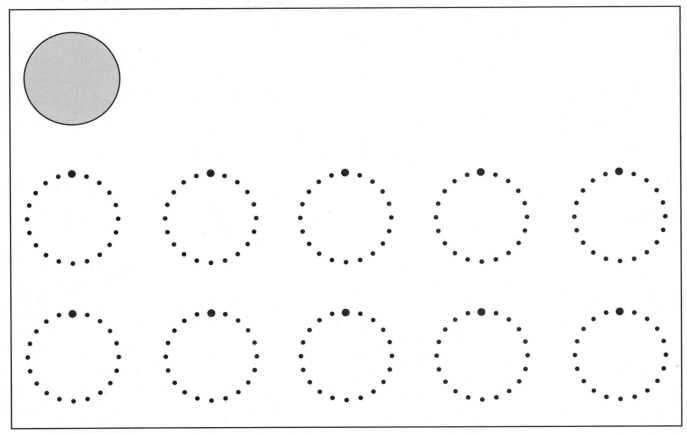

"What shape did you draw?" "Show me how you drew it."

Side 2 _____

Lesson 88   Name _____

"Where did you put the cat?" "Where did you put the mouse?" "Where did you put the dog?" "Where did you put the turtle?"

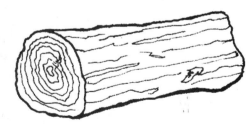

"What is on the long log?" "What is on the short log?"

Side 1 _____

Lesson 88   Name _____

"Where does the food go?" "Where do the containers go?"

Point to a triangle. "What is this?" "What color is it?" Point to a rectangle. "What is this?" "What color is it?"

Side 2 _____

Lesson 89   Name _____

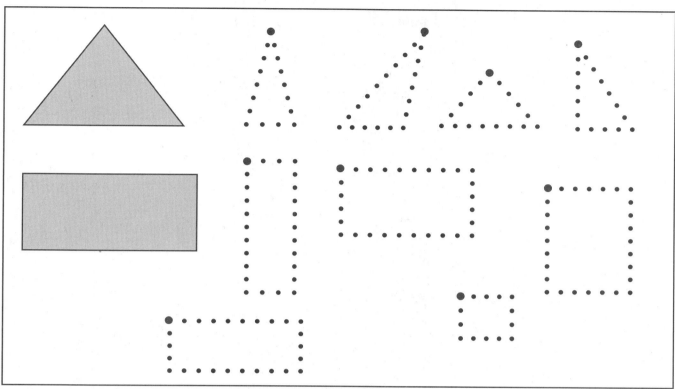

"Show me a triangle you drew." "Show me a rectangle you drew."

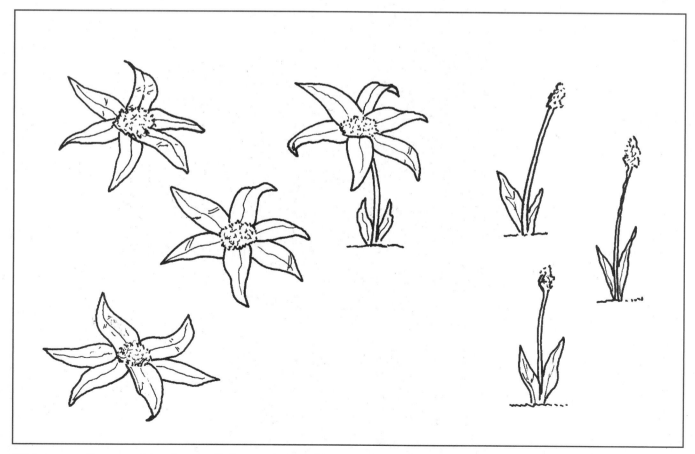

"Show me a line you drew from a flower to a stem."

Side 1 _____

Lesson 89

Name _____

Point to a vehicle. "What is it?" "What color is it?" Point to a food. "What is it?" "What color is it?"

"Tell me where you put the mouse." "Tell me where you put the cat." "Tell me where you put the squirrel."
"Tell me where you put the bird."

Lesson 90   Name _____

"Tell me where you put the dog." "Tell me where you put the cat." "Tell me where you put the girl."

"What is under the tall horse?" "What did you draw under the short horse?"

Side 1 _____

Lesson 90   Name _____

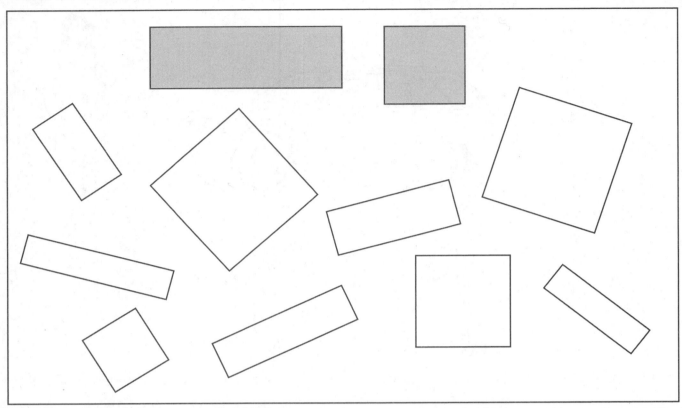

Point to a square. "What is this?" "What color is it?"

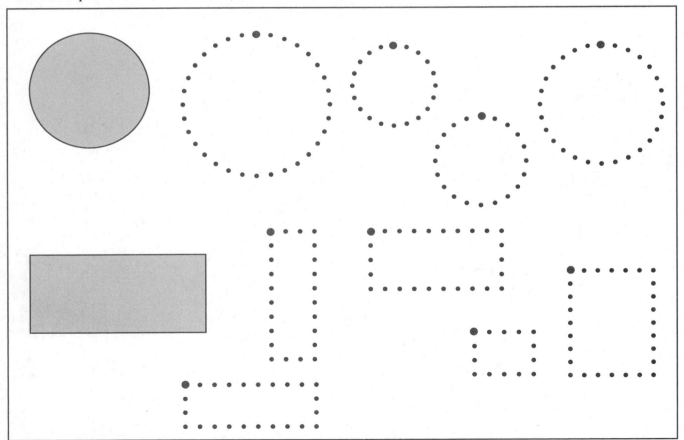

"Show me how you drew a circle." "Show me how you drew a rectangle."

Side 2 _____

Lesson 91   Name _____

"Tell me which house you put the big pigs in." "Tell me which house you put the small pigs in."

"Point to a vehicle." "What color is it?" "Point to some food." "What color is it?"

Lesson 91   Name _____

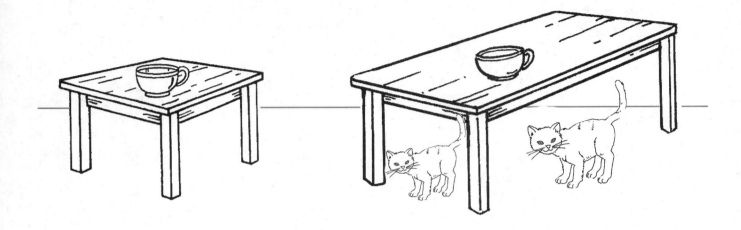

"Show me the long table." "What is under it?" "What did you draw under the short table?"

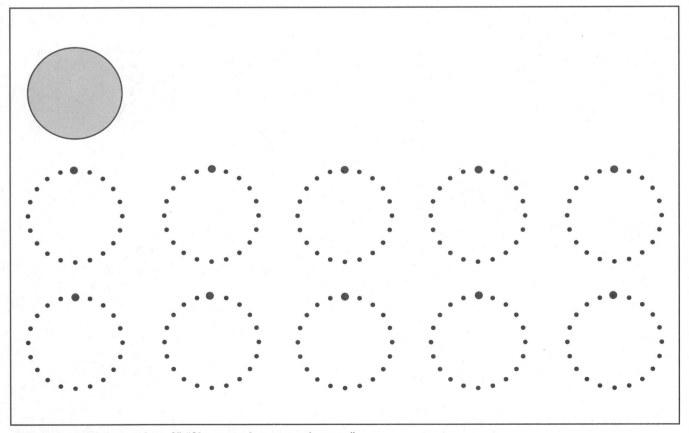

"What shape did you draw?" "Show me how you drew it."

Lesson 92   Name _____

"Tell me which house you put the big cats in." "Tell me which house you put the small cats in."

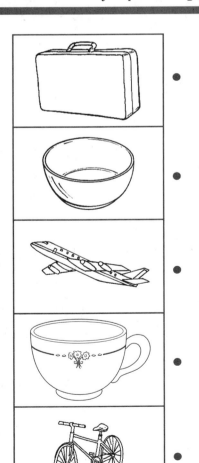 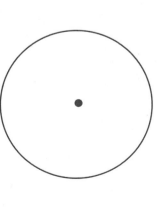 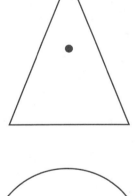   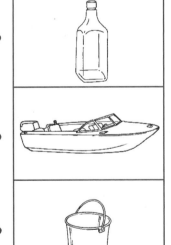

"Where do the containers go?" "Where do the vehicles go?"

Side 1 _____

Lesson 92   Name _____

"Show me the dog that is wet." "Show me the dog that is dry."

Point to a circle. "What is this?" "What color is it?" Point to a rectangle. "What is this?" "What color is it?"

Side 2 _____

Lesson 93   Name _____

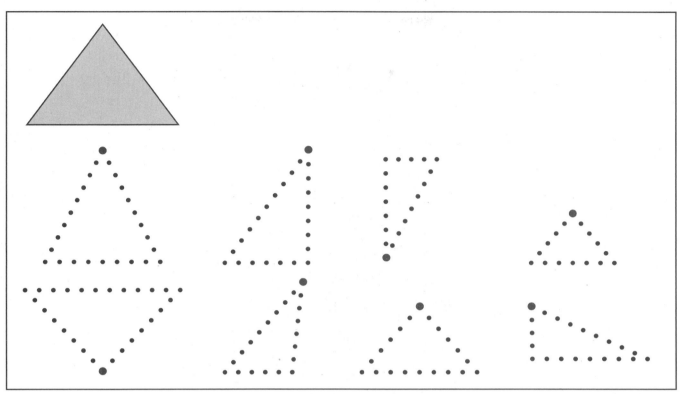

"What shape did you draw?" "Show me how you drew it."

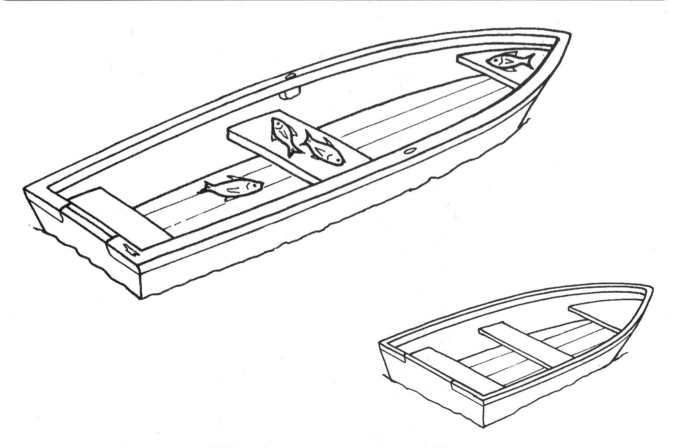

"Tell me what is in the long boat." "What did you draw in the short boat?"

Side 1 _____

Lesson 93   Name _____

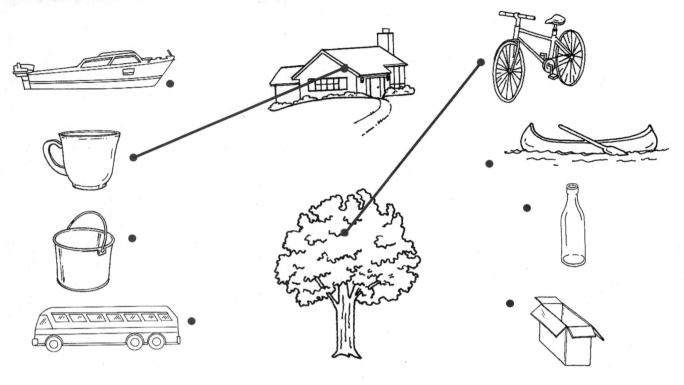

"Tell me what you put in the house." "Tell me what you put in the tree."

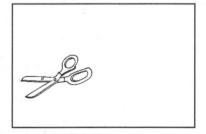

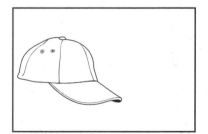

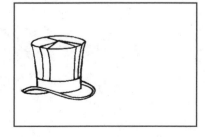

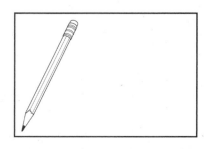

"Touch a box you circled." "What's in the box?" "What did you draw?" "Touch another box you circled." "What's in the box?" "What did you draw?"

Side 2 _____

Lesson 94   Name _____

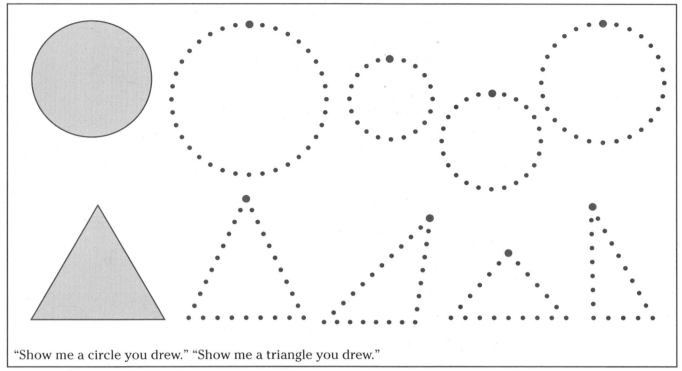

"Show me a circle you drew." "Show me a triangle you drew."

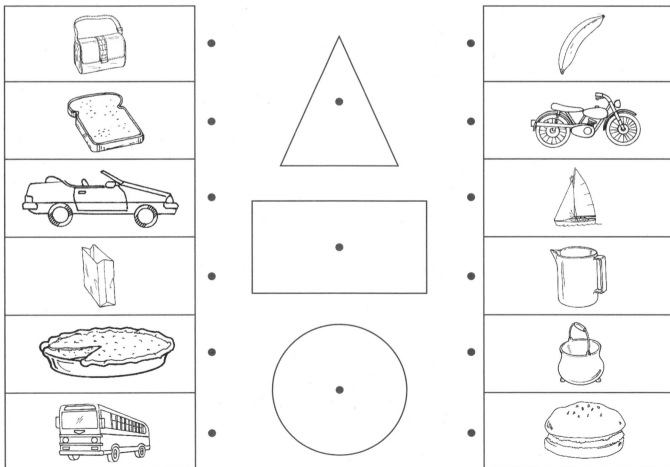

"What kind of objects go in the triangle?" "What kind of objects go in the rectangle?" "What kind of objects go in the circle?"

Side 1 _____

Lesson 94   Name _____

"Show me a big animal." "What is it?" "What color is it?" "Show me a small animal." "What is it?"
"What color is it?"

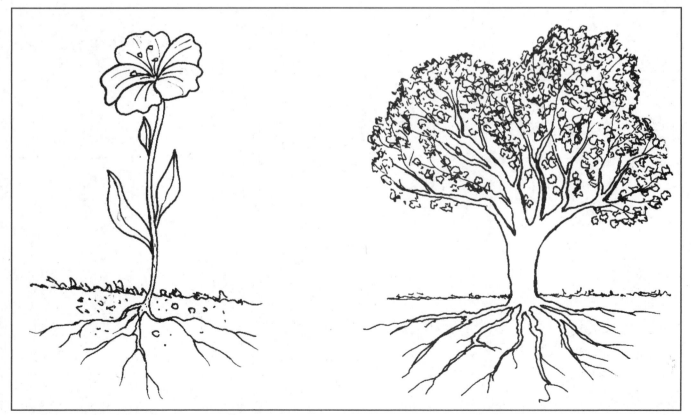

"Tell me the parts of the flower." "Tell me the parts of the tree."

Side 2 _____

Lesson 95   Name _____

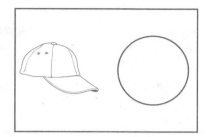

  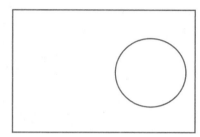

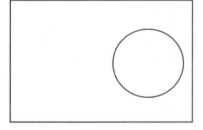 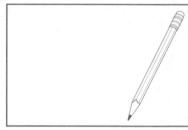 

"What's in the top box?" "Show me a box that is not crossed out." "What is in it?" "What did you draw?"

"Where is the yellow rabbit?" "Where is the black rabbit?"

Side 1 _____

Lesson 95   Name _____

"Show me an object that is black." "What kind of object is it?" "Show me an object that is red." "What kind of object is it?"

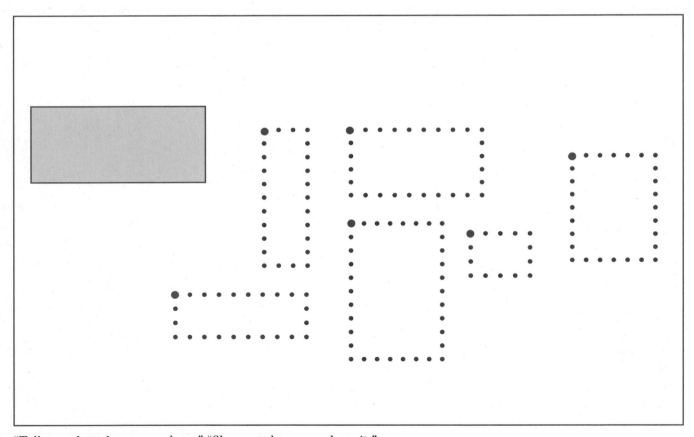

"Tell me what shape you drew." "Show me how you drew it."

Side 2 _____

Lesson 96   Name _____

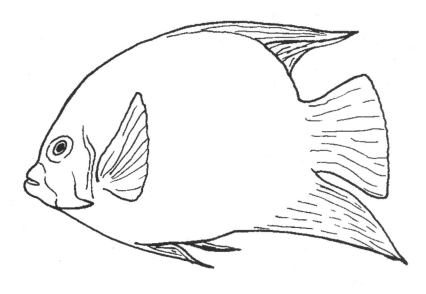
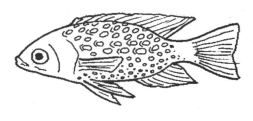

"What was missing from the big fish?" "What did you draw?"

"What's in the top box?" "Show me a box that is not crossed out." "What's in it?" "What did you draw?"

Side 1 _____

Lesson 96   Name _____

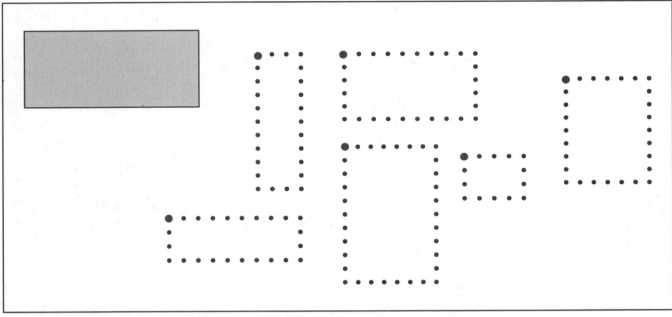

"Tell me what shape you drew." "Show me how you drew it."

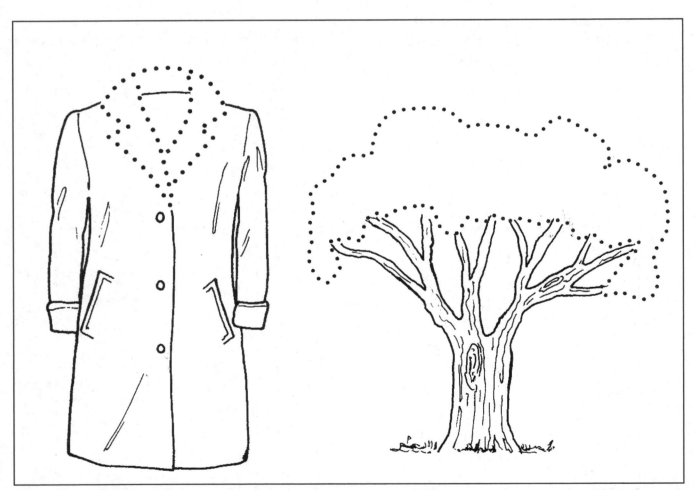

"What was missing from the coat?" "Show me how you drew it." "What was missing from the tree?" "Show me how you drew it."

Side 2 _____

Lesson 97   Name _____

"Show me a full container." "What color is it?" "Show me an empty container." "What color is it?"

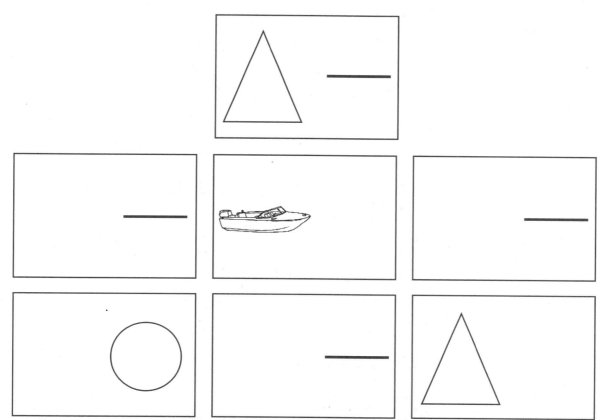

"What's in the top box?" "Show me a box that is not crossed out?" "What's in it?" "What did you draw?"

Side 1 _____

Lesson 97   Name _____

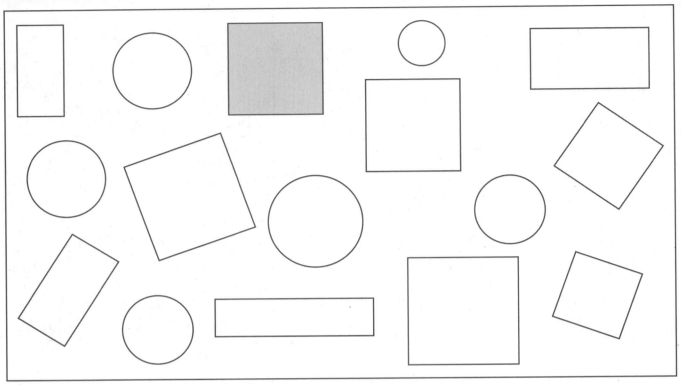

Point to a square. "What is it?" "What color is it?" Point to a circle. "What is it?" "What color is it?" Point to a rectangle. "What is it?" "What color is it?"

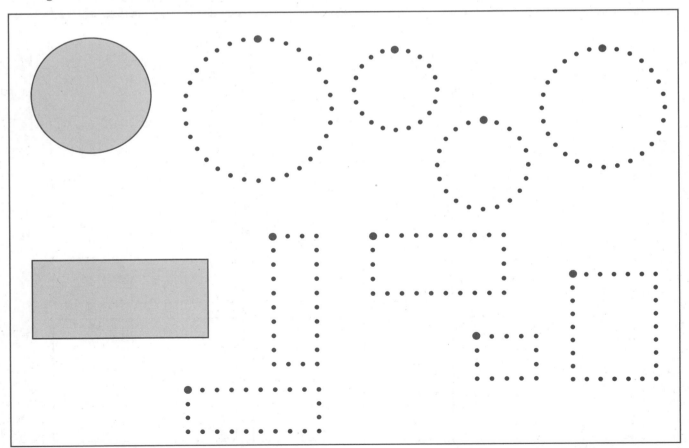

"What shapes did you draw?" "Show me how you drew a circle." "Show me how you drew a rectangle."

Side 2 _____

Lesson 98   Name _____

"What did you draw on the dry cat?" "Touch the other cat." "Is it wet or dry?"

"Show me a short log." "What color is it?" "Show me a long log." "What color is it?"

Side 1 _____

Lesson 98   Name _____

"What kind of objects did you color black?" "What kind of objects did you color green?"

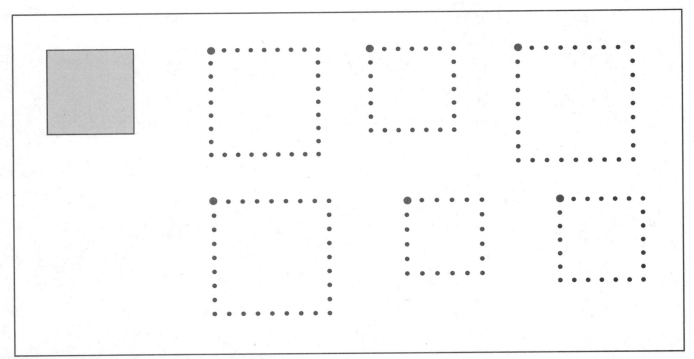

"What shape did you draw?" "Show me how you drew it."

Side 2 _____

Lesson 99

Name _____

"Show me a brown object." "What is it made of?" "Show me a yellow object." "What is it made of?" "What part did you draw to finish the spoon?"

"Which container do the small cats drink from?" "Which container do the big cats drink from?"

Side 1 _____

Lesson 99   Name _____

"What color are the dry dogs?" "What color are the wet dogs?"

"What is in the circle?" "Which objects belong in the circle?"

Lesson 100   Name _____

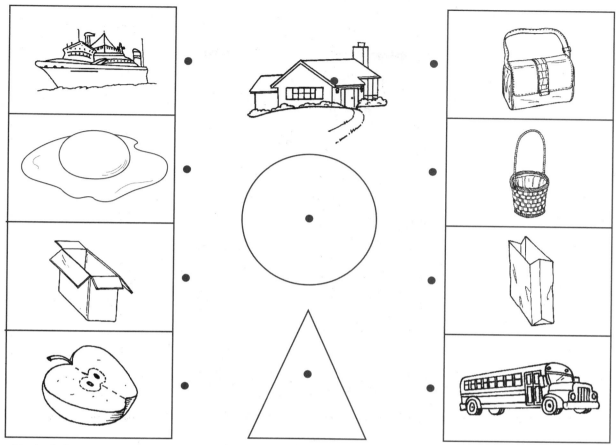

"What kind of objects go in the house?" "What kind of objects go in the circle?" "What kind of objects go in the triangle?"

"What color are the dry horses?" "What color are the wet horses?"

Side 1 _____

Lesson 100   Name _____

"What kind of objects did you color purple?" "What kind did you color red?" "What did you draw to finish the shirt?"

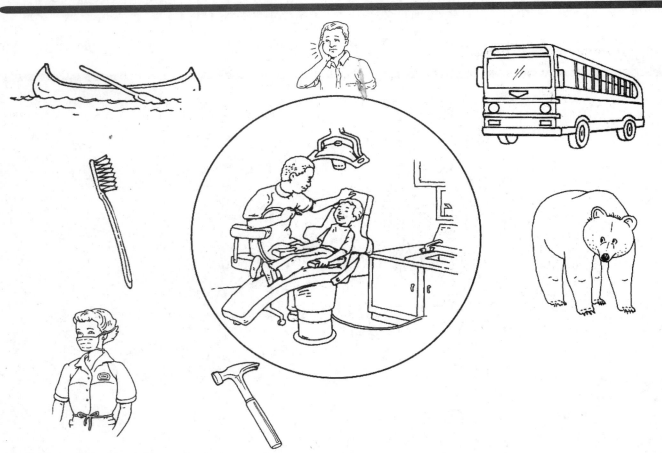

"What is in the circle?" "Tell me which objects belong in the circle."

Side 2 _____

Lesson 101   Name _____

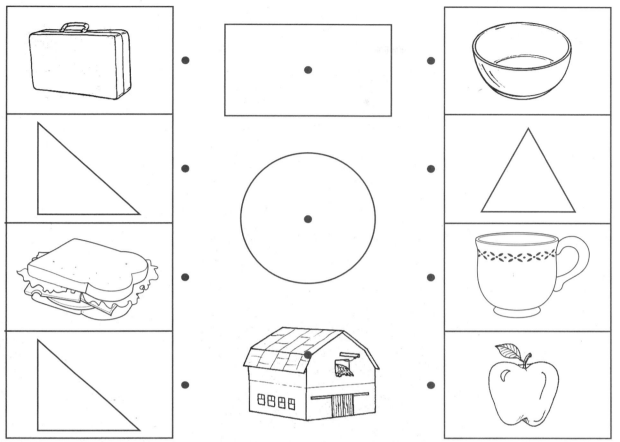

"Where do the containers go?" "Where do the triangles go?" "Where does the food go?"

"Tell me where the red containers are." "Tell me where the blue containers are." "Tell me where the yellow containers are."

Side 1 _____

Lesson 101   Name _____

"What is in the circle?" "Tell me which objects belong in the circle." "Tell me which objects do not belong in the circle."

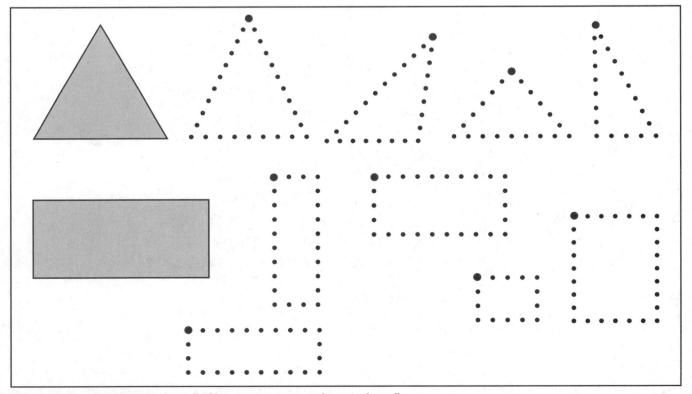

"Show me a triangle you drew." "Show me a rectangle you drew."

Side 2 _____

Lesson 102   Name _____

"What kind of objects go in the barn?" "What kind of objects go in the house?" "What kind of objects go in the tree?"

"Tell me where the yellow animal is." "What is it?" "Tell me where the black animal is." "What is it?"

Side 1 _____

Lesson 102   Name _____

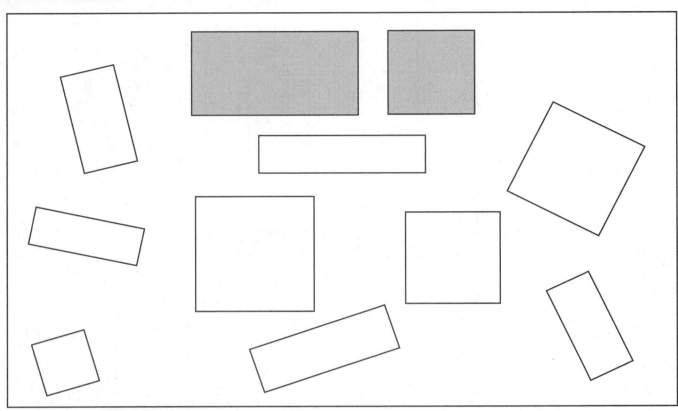

"Point to all the squares in the picture." "What color are they?"

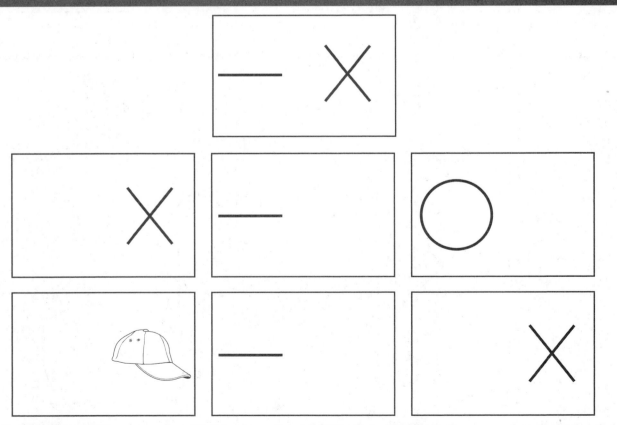

"What's in the box?" "Show me a box that is crossed out." "What's in it?" "Now show me a box that is not crossed out." "What did you draw?"

Side 2 _____

Lesson 103   Name _____

"What color are the vehicles?" "What color are the animals?"

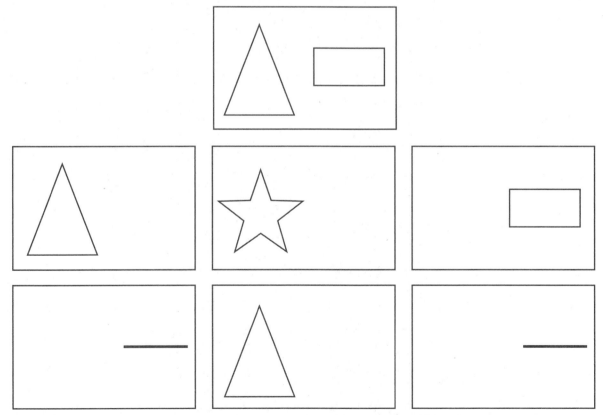

"What's in the top box?" "Show me a box that is crossed out." "What's in it?" "Now show me a box that is not crossed out." "What did you draw?"

Side 1 _____

Lesson 103   Name _____

"Which animals go in back of the car?" "Which animal goes on top of the car?" "Which animal goes in front of the car?"

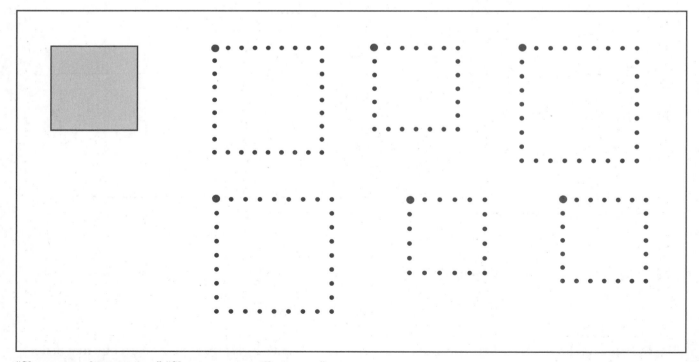

"Show me a big square." "Show me a small square."

Side 2 _____

Lesson 104   Name _____

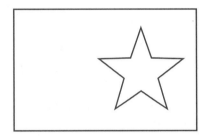

"What's in the top box?" "Show me a box that is crossed out." "What's in it?" "Show me a box that is not crossed out." "What did you draw?"

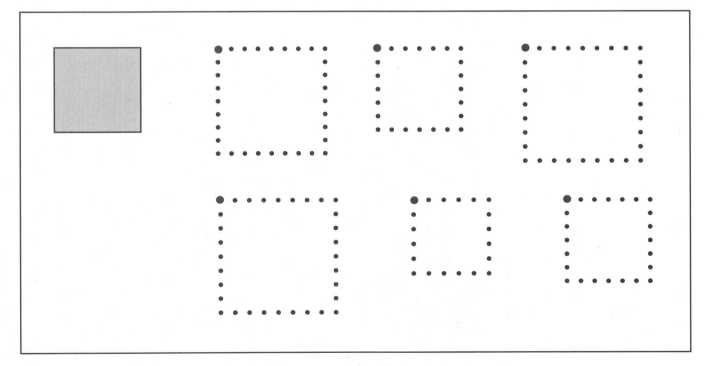

"Show me how you drew a small square." "Show me how you drew a big square."

Side 1 _____

Lesson 104   Name _____

"What color are the wet dogs?" "What color are the dry dogs?"

"Show me something that is made of wood." "What is it?" "Show me something that is not made of wood."
"What is it?"

Side 2 _____

Lesson 105   Name _____

"What color did you make the rectangles?" "What color did you make the triangles?"

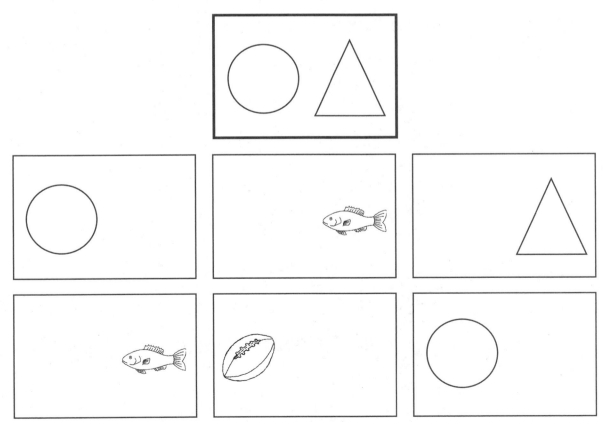

"What's in the top box?" "Show me a box that is crossed out." "What's in it?" "Show me a box that is not crossed out." "What did you draw?"

Side 1 _____

Lesson 105   Name _____

"Show me a full container." "What color is it?" "Show me an empty container." "What color is it?"

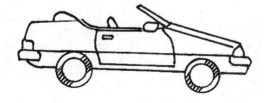  

"Show me something that is made of metal." "What is it?" "Show me something that is not made of metal." "What is it?"

Side 2 _____

Lesson 106 Name _____

"What color are the buldings?" "What color are the vehicles?"

"Show me how you drew the missing parts of the rectangles." "What color are they?"

Side 1 _____

Lesson 106   Name _____

"What color is the animal that's between the boys?" "What is it?" "What color are the animals that are in back of the boys?" "What are they?"

"Show me something that's made of cloth." "What is it?" "Show me something that is not made of cloth." "What is it?"

Side 2 _____

Lesson 107   Name _____

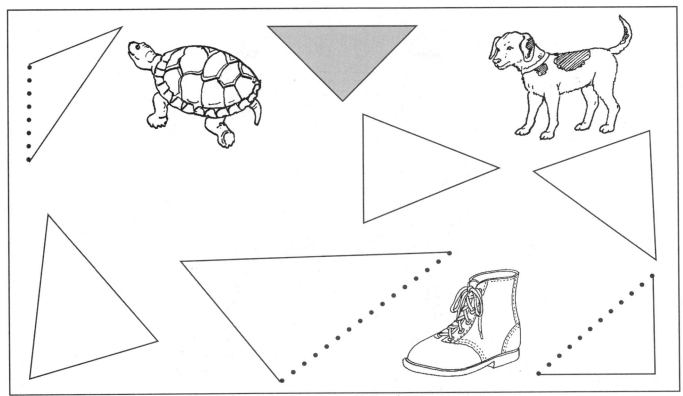

"Show me how you drew the missing parts of the triangles." "What color are they?"

"Show me something that's made of leather." "What is it?" "Show me something that's not made of leather."
"What is it?"

Side 1 _____

Lesson 107   Name _____

"What kind of objects did you color yellow?" "What kind of objects did you color green?"

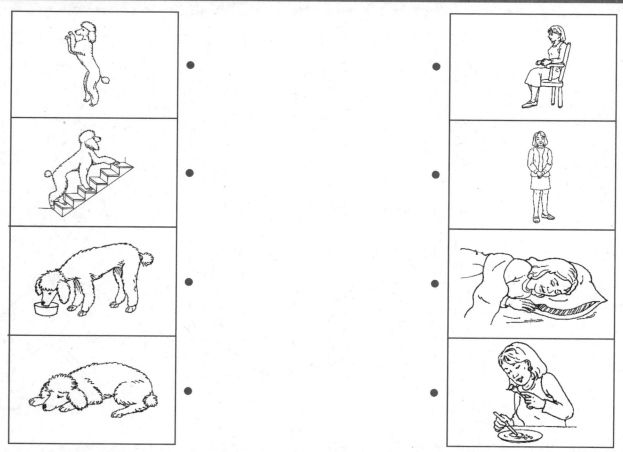

"Show me the pictures where the dog and the woman are doing the same thing." "What are they doing?"

Side 2 _____

Lesson 108

Name _____

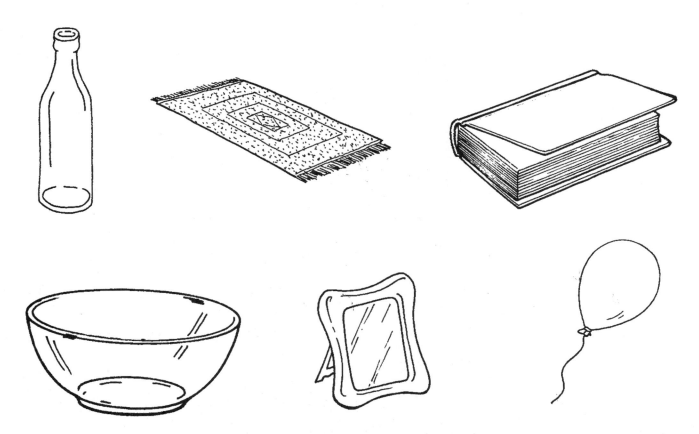

"Show me something that's made of glass." "What is it?" "Show me something that's not made of glass." "What is it?"

"What parts of the table did you draw?" "What color are they?"

Side 1 _____

Lesson 108   Name  _____

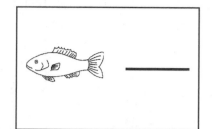 _____

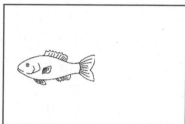 _____      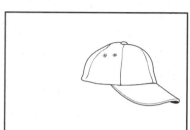

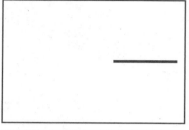      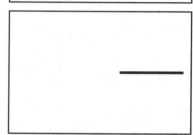 _____

"What's in the top box?" "Show me a box that is crossed out." "What's in it?" "Show me a box that's not crossed out." "What did you draw?"

   •   • 

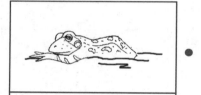   •   • 

  •   • 

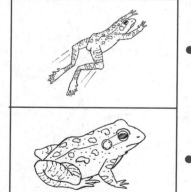   •   • 

"Show me a line that connects a dog and a frog." "What are they doing?" Repeat for all pairs.

Side 2 _____

Lesson 109   Name _____

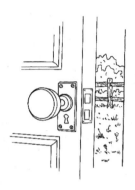

"Show me something that's made of cloth." "What is it?" "Show me something that's not made of cloth." "What is it?"

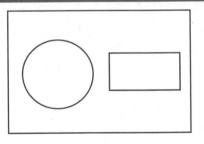

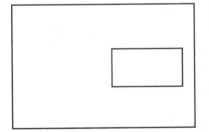

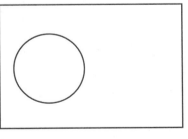

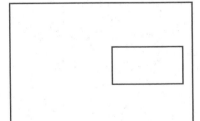
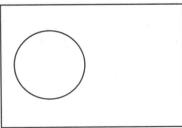

"What's in the top box?" "Show me a box that's crossed out." "What's in it?" "Show me a box that's not crossed out." "What did you draw?"

Side 1 _____

Lesson 109   Name _____

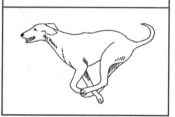

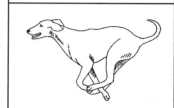

"What are the dogs doing?" "What are the boys doing?" "What are the girls doing?"

"Show me a basket that's not empty." "What did you draw on it?" "Show me a basket that is empty." "What part is missing?"

Side 2 _____

Lesson 110   Name _____

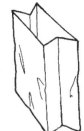

"Show me something that's made of paper." "What is it?" "Show me something that's not made of paper." "What is it?"

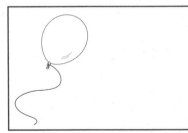

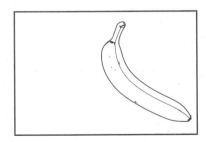

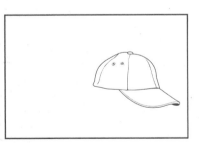

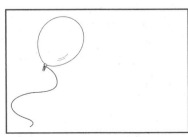
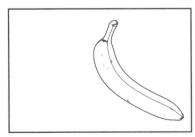

"What's in the top box?" "Show me a box that's crossed out." "What's in it?" "Show me a box that's not crossed out." "What did you draw?"

Side 1 _____

Lesson 110   Name _____

"Where are the green birds?" "Where is the blue bird?"

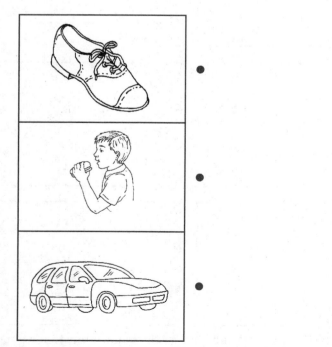

"Look at the objects connected by a green line." "How are they the same?" Repeat for brown and blue lines.

Side 2 _____

Lesson 111   Name _____

 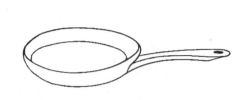 

 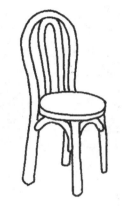 

"Show me something that's made of wood." "What is it?" "Show me something that's not made of wood." "What is it?"

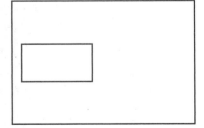

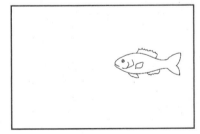 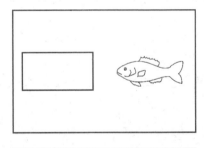

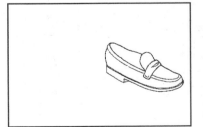  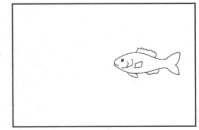

"What's in the top box?" "Show me a box that's crossed out." "What's in it?" "Show me a box that's not crossed out." "What did you draw?"

Side 1 _____

Lesson 111   Name _____

"Tell me what you colored blue." "Tell me what you colored green."

"What color are the tall trees?" "What color are the short trees?"

Side 2 _____

Lesson 112   Name _____

"Which animal is black?" "Which animal is red?" "Which animal is orange?" "What is the other animal?"

"Show me the containers." "What color are they?" "Show me the plants." "What color are they?"

Side 1 _____

Lesson 112   Name _____

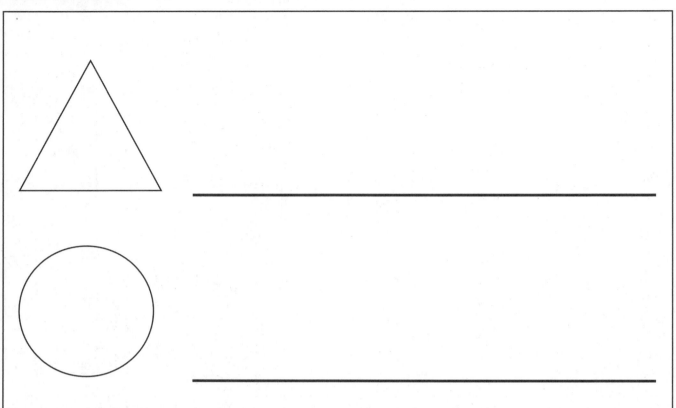

"Tell me the names of the shapes you drew."

"Look at the objects connected by a red line." "How are they the same?" Repeat for blue and black lines.

Side 2 _____

Lesson 113   Name _____

"What color did you make the coat?"

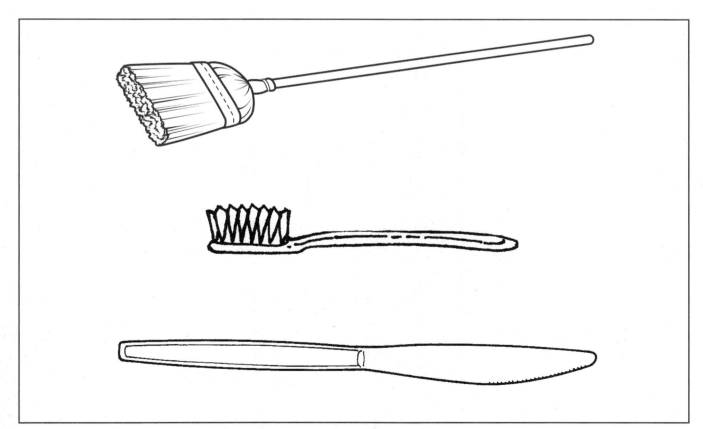

"What part of the objects did you color orange?" "What part of the objects did you color yellow?"

Side 1 _____

Lesson 113   Name _____

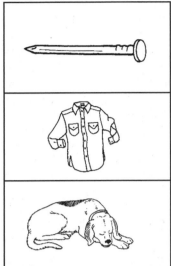

"Look at the objects connected by a blue line." "How are they the same?" Repeat for brown and green lines.

"Tell me what you colored red." "Tell me what you colored black." "Tell me what you colored brown."

Side 2 _____

Lesson 114   Name _____

"What color is the rabbit?" "What color is the lion?" "What color is the bear?" "What is the other animal?"

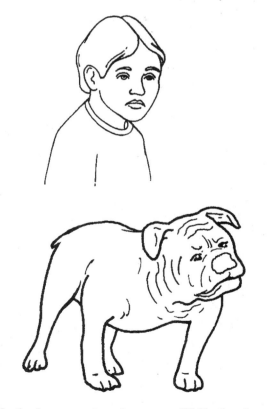

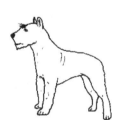

"Is the boy wearing glasses sad?" "Is the dog with the long tail big?"

Side 1 _____

Lesson 114   Name _____

"What did you color black?" "What did you color green?" "What did you color yellow?" "What did you color red?"

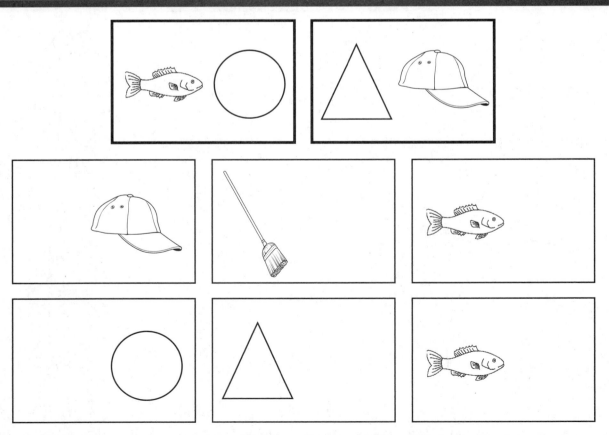

"Tell me what's in the top two boxes." "Tell me what you drew to fix the other boxes."

Lesson 115   Name _____

"What color is the bowl?" "What color is the glass?" "What color is the plate?" "What else is on the table?"

"Tell me what's in the top two boxes." "Tell me what you drew to fix the other boxes."

Side 1 _____

Lesson 115   Name _____

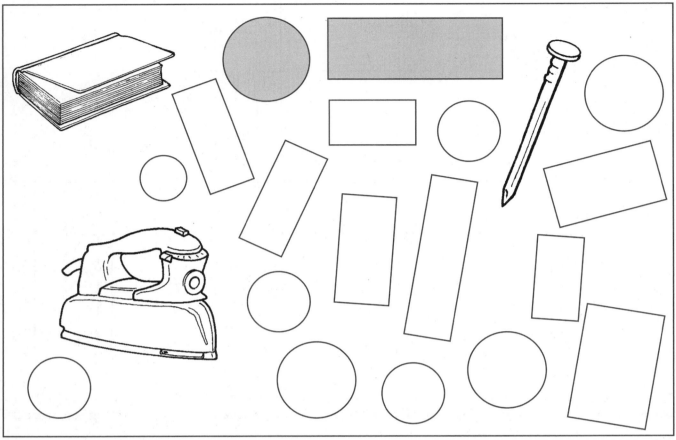

"What rule did you make for rectangles?" "What rule did you make for circles?"

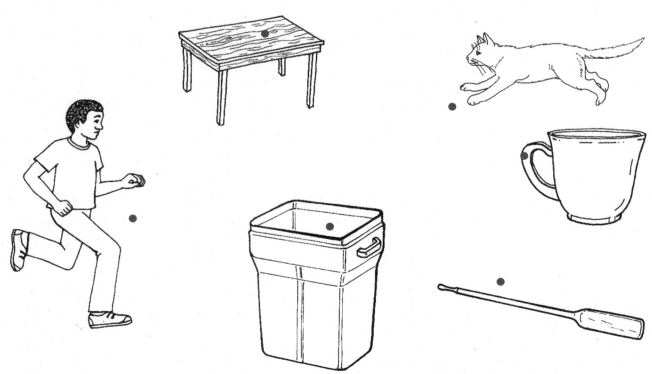

"Look at the objects connected by a brown line." "How are they the same?" Repeat for green and blue lines.

Side 2 _____

Lesson 116   Name _____

"What was missing from the wagon?" "What part of the wagon is blue?" "What part is black?"

"Tell me what you colored blue." "Tell me what you colored yellow." "Tell me what you colored black."

Lesson 116   Name _____

"What did you color brown?" "What did you color pink?" "Tell me what objects you crossed out."

"What's in the top two boxes?" "Tell me what you drew to fix the other boxes." "What did you cross out?"

Side 2 _____

Lesson 117   Name _____

"What color did you make the boy's shirt?"

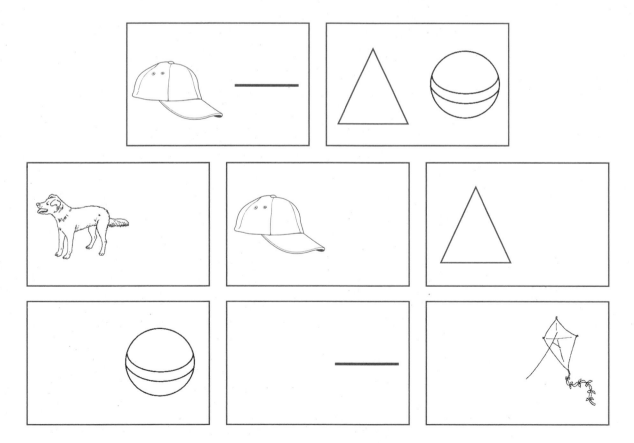

"What's in the top two boxes?" "Tell me what you drew to fix up the other boxes." "What did you cross out?"

Side 1 _____

Lesson 117

Name _____

"Look at the objects connected by a red line." "How are they the same?" Repeat for brown and orange lines.

"Is the cat with the hat striped?" "Is the dog with the collar sitting?"

Side 2 _____

Lesson 118   Name _____

"What color are the rectangles?" "Show me how you followed the dots."

"What color is the shoe?" "What color is the shirt?" "What color is the hat?" "What else is in the picture?"

Side 1 _____

Lesson 118   Name _____

  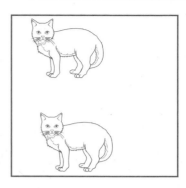

  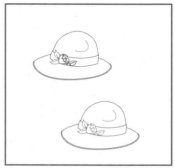

"What did you color red?" "What did you color brown?" "What did you color yellow?"

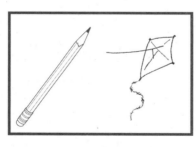 

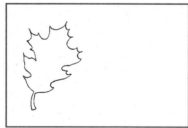  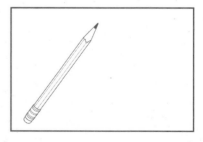

"What's in the top two boxes?" "Tell me what you drew to fix up the other boxes." "What did you cross out?"

Side 2 _____

Lesson 119   Name _____

"What did you color blue?" "Is it full or empty?" "What did you color red?" "Is it full or empty?"

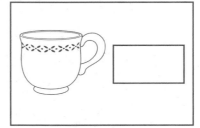

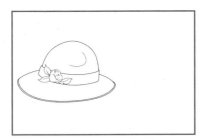

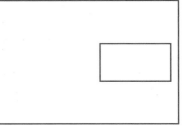

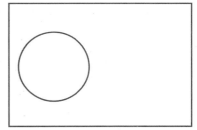

"What's in the top two boxes?" "Tell me what you drew to fix up the other boxes." "What did you cross out?"

Side 1 _____

Lesson 119   Name _____

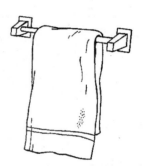

"Look at the two objects connected by a black line." "How are they the same?" Repeat for brown and green lines.

"Tell me where the orange vehicle is." "What is it?" "Tell me where the brown vehicle is." "What is it?"

Side 2 _____

Lesson 120   Name _____

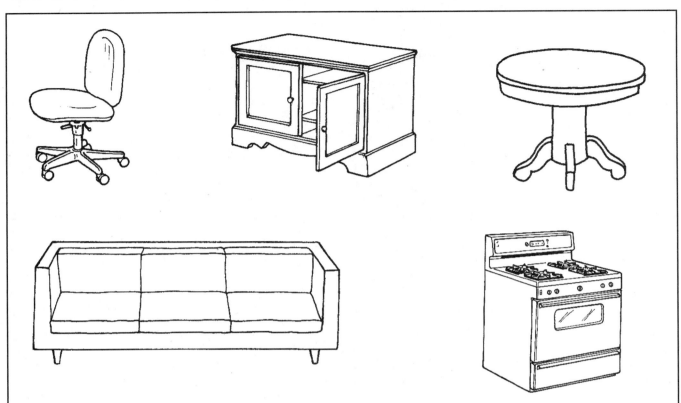

"What color is the table?" "What color is the chair?" "What color is the couch?" "What else is in the picture?"

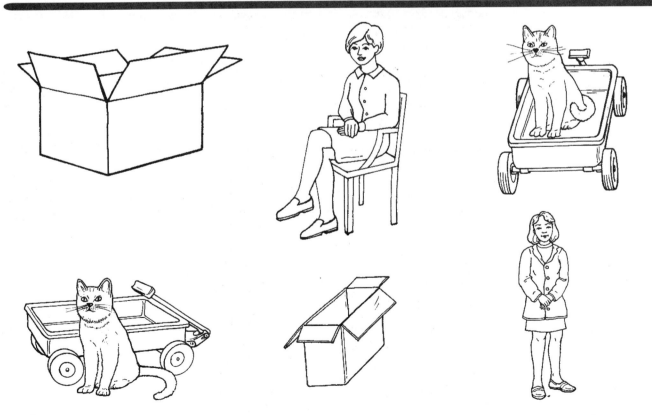

"Is the woman in the red coat sitting?" "Is the box with a cross-out mark big?" "Is the cat next to the wagon wearing a collar?"

Side 1 _____

Lesson 120   Name _____

"What part of the umbrella was missing?" "What color did you make it?" "What part of the umbrella is brown?" "What part is orange?"

"What's in the top two boxes?" "Tell me what you drew to fix up the other boxes." "What did you cross out?"

Side 2 _____

Lesson 121   Name _____

"Show me a long log." "What color is it?" "Show me a short log." "What color is it?"

"What's in the top two boxes?" "Tell me what you drew to fix the other boxes." "What did you cross out?"

Side 1 _____

Lesson 121   Name _____

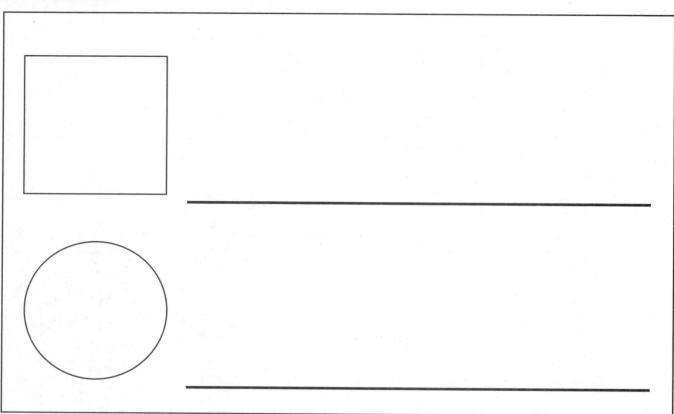

"What shape did you draw on the top line?" "What shape did you draw on the bottom line?"

"Look at the objects connected by a pink line." "How are they the same?" Repeat for blue, brown, and green lines.

Side 2 _____

Lesson 122   Name _____

"Tell me what kind of objects you colored red." "Tell me what kind of objects you colored green."

"Tell me the parts of the flower." "Which part was missing?"

Side 1 _____

Lesson 122   Name _____

"What's in the top two boxes?" "Tell me what you drew to fix the other boxes." "What did you cross out?"

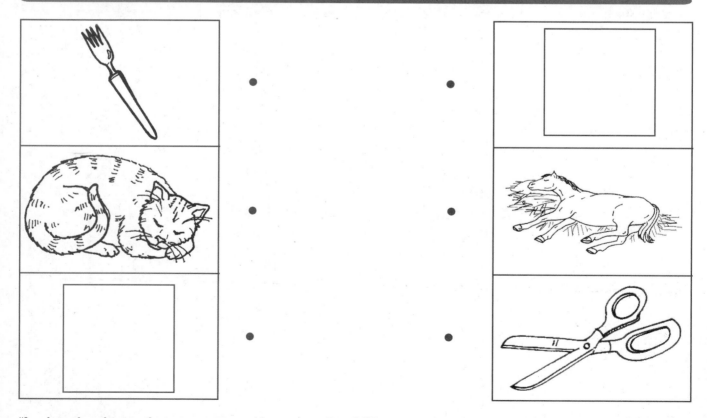

"Look at the objects that are connected by a green line." "How are they the same?" Repeat for brown and blue lines.

Side 2 _____

Lesson 123 Name _____

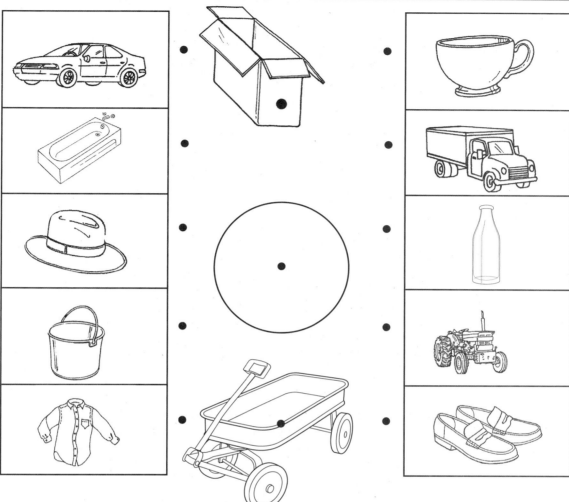

"Tell me what kind of objects you put in the box." Repeat for circle and wagon.

"Is the woman in the red coat sitting?" "Is the box with a cross-out mark on it big?" "Is the orange cat next to the wagon?"

Side 1 _____

Lesson 123   Name _____

"Tell me the parts of the coat." "Which part was missing?"

"What kind of objects did you draw circles around?" "What kind of objects did you draw triangles around?
"What objects are left over?"

Side 2 _____

Lesson 124   Name _____

"Tell me what kind of objects you colored purple." "Tell me what kind of objects you colored brown."

"Does the lumberjack with the red jacket have a long axe?" "Are his boots short?" "Does the lumberjack with the black boots have a short axe?"

Lesson 124   Name _____

"What's in the top two boxes?" "Tell me what you drew to fix the other boxes." "What did you cross out?"

"Look at the objects connected by an orange line." "How are they the same?" Repeat for brown and yellow lines.

Side 2 _____

Lesson 125   Name _____

"Tell me where the yellow objects are." "Tell me where the red objects are." "Tell me where the brown object is."

"What kind of objects did you circle?" "What kind of objects did you draw squares around?" "What objects are left over?"

Side 1 _____

Lesson 125   Name _____

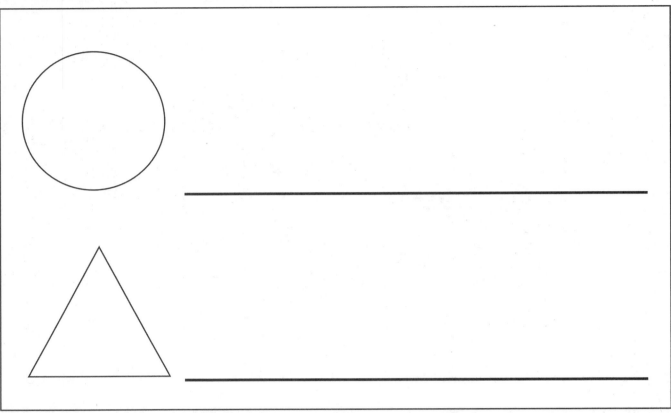

"What shape did you draw on the top line?" "What shape did you draw on the bottom line?"

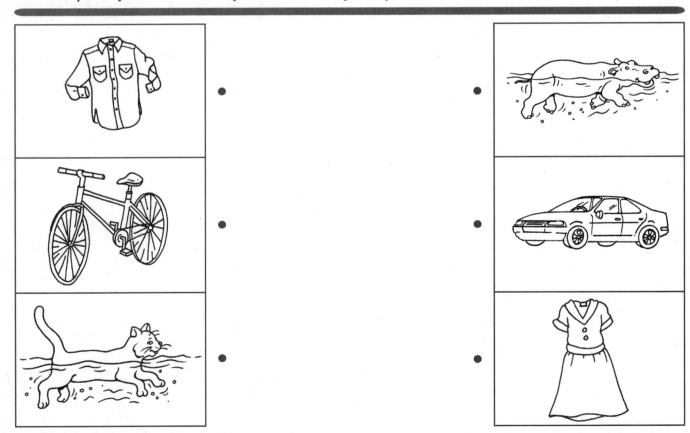

"Look at the objects connected by the brown line." "How are they the same?" Repeat for blue and red lines.

Side 2 _____

Lesson 126   Name _____

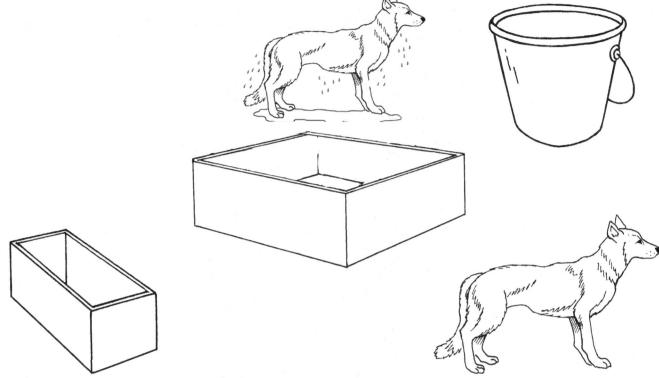

"Is the box with a circle on it big?" "Is the dog that's wearing a collar wet?" "Does the box with a bird on it also have a circle on it?"

"What rule did you make for the circles?" "What rule did you make for the triangles?"

Side 1 _____

Lesson 126   Name _____

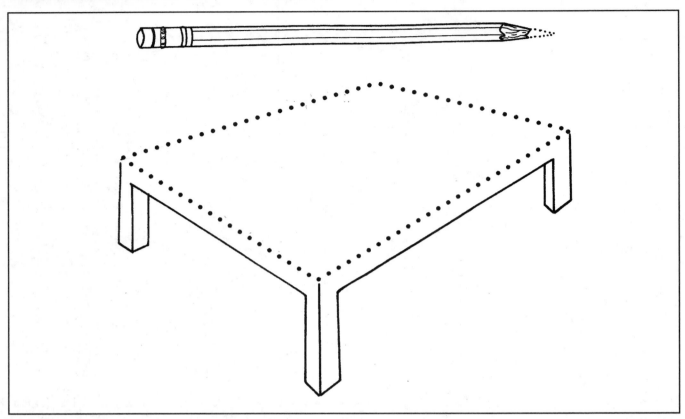

"Which part of the pencil was missing?" "Which part of the table was missing?"

"What's in the top two boxes?" "Tell me what you drew to fix the other boxes." "What did you cross out?"

Side 2 _____

Lesson 127　　Name _____

"What color are the tall trees?" "What color are the short trees?"

"What kind of objects did you draw rectangles around?" "What kind of objects did you draw triangles around?"

Side 1 _____

Lesson 127   Name _____

"What's in the top two boxes?" "Tell me what you drew to fix the other boxes." "What did you cross out?"

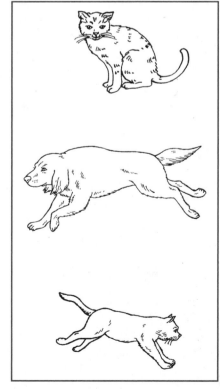

"What's the same about the connected objects in the first box?" "What did you cross out?" Repeat for second and third boxes.

Side 2 _____

Lesson 128   Name _____

"Does the lumberjack wearing green pants have a long axe?" "Is the lumberjack with the black jacket wearing short boots?" "Does the lumberjack with brown boots have a long axe?"

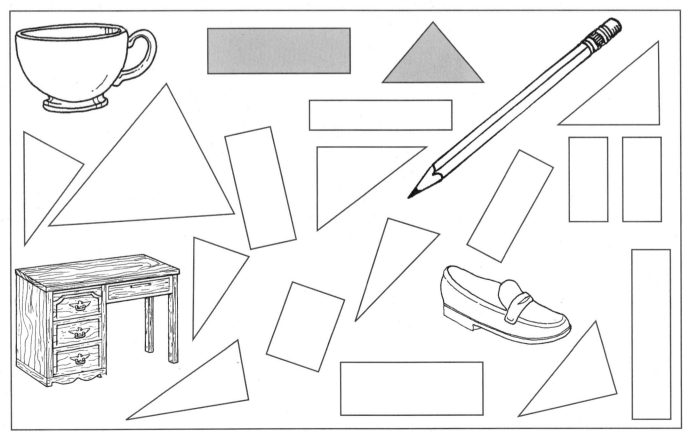

"What rule did you make for the rectangles?" "What rule did you make for the triangles?"

Side 1 _____

Lesson 128   Name _____

"Tell me the parts of the house." "Which part was missing?"

"Where are the blue birds?" "How many birds are next to the car?" "Where are the red birds?"

Side 2 _____

Lesson 129   Name _____

"What kind of objects did you color orange?" "What kind of objects did you color brown?"

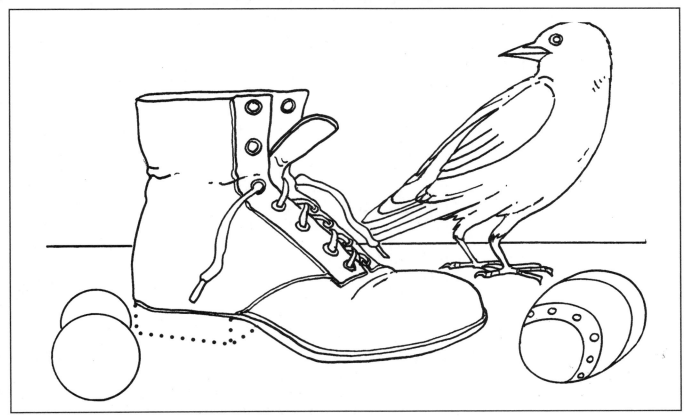

"Tell me the parts of the shoe." "Which part was missing?"

Side 1 _____

Lesson 129　Name _____

"What's in the top two boxes?" "Tell me what you drew to fix the other boxes." "What did you cross out?"

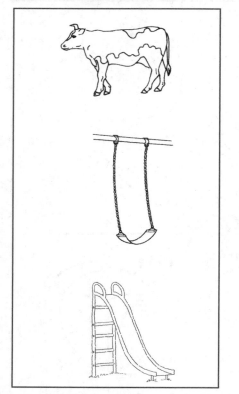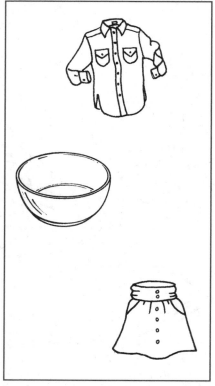

"What's the same about the connected objects in the first box?" "What did you cross out?" Repeat for second and third boxes.

Side 2 _____

Lesson 130   Name _____

"What animals did you color black?" "What animals did you color red?"

"What kind of objects did you circle?" "What kind of objects did you draw squares around?"

Side 1 _____

Lesson 130   Name _____

"Is the firefighter wearing goggles dry?" "Is the firefighter wearing blue sitting on a short bench?" "Is the firefighter with an axe next to him wet?"

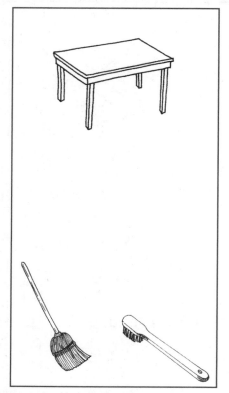 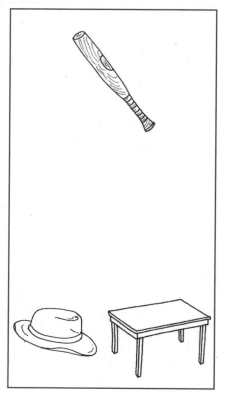 

"What's the same about the connected objects in the first box?" "What did you cross out?" Repeat for second and third boxes.

Side 2 _____

Lesson 131　 Name _____

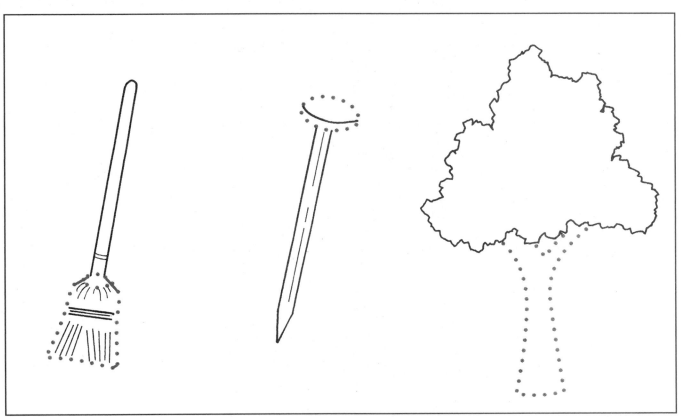

"Show me the broom." "Which part did you draw?" Repeat for nail and tree.

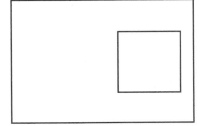

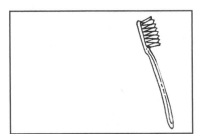

"What's in the top two boxes?" "Tell me what you drew to fix the other boxes." "What did you cross out?"

Side 1 _____

Lesson 131   Name _____

"What's in the circle?" "Name the objects that belong in the circle." "Name the ones that don't belong."

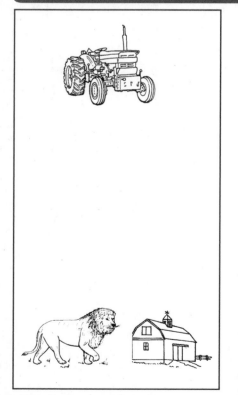 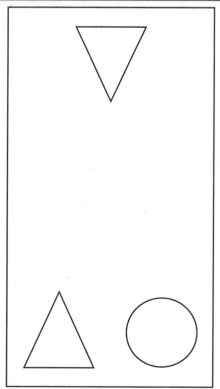 

"What's the same about the connected objects in the first box?" "What did you cross out?" Repeat for second and third boxes.

Side 2 _____

Lesson 132   Name _____

"What did you color yellow?" "What did you color blue?"

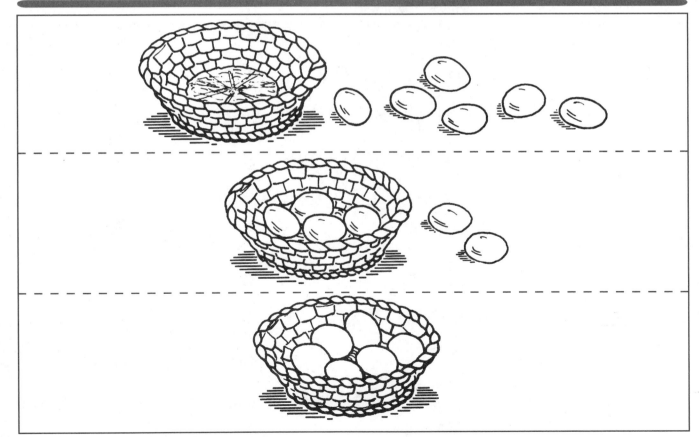

"Find the picture with <u>some</u> of the eggs in the basket." "Find the picture with <u>all</u> of the eggs in the basket."
"Find the picture with <u>none</u> of the eggs in the basket."

Side 1 _____

Lesson 132   Name _____

"Tell me the parts of the chair." "Which part was missing?"

"What kind of objects did you color red?"

Side 2 _____

Lesson 133   Name _____

"Find the picture with <u>all</u> of the dogs in the doghouse." "Find the picture with <u>none</u> of the dogs in the doghouse." "Find the picture with <u>some</u> of the dogs in the doghouse."

"Which part of the broom did you draw?"

Side 1 _____

Lesson 133   Name _____

"Tell me which objects are red." "Tell me which are brown." "Tell me which are yellow."

"What's in the circle?" "Name the objects that belong in the circle." "Name the ones that don't belong."

Lesson 134   Name _____

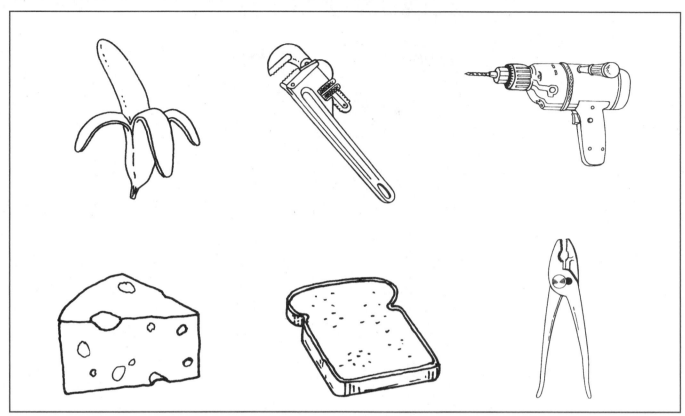

"What kind of objects did you draw triangles around?" "What kind of objects did you circle?"

"Tell me the parts of the wagon." "Which part of the wagon was missing?"

Lesson 134   Name _____

"What's in the top two boxes?" "Tell me what you drew to fix the other boxes." "What did you cross out?"

"What kind of objects are pink?" "What are the other objects?"

Lesson 135   Name _____

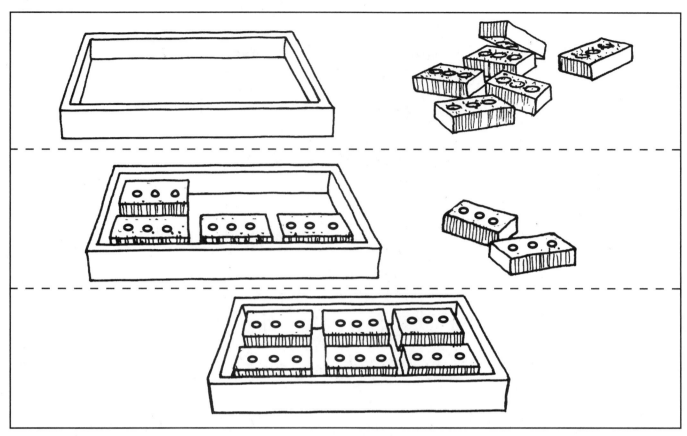

"Find the picture with <u>some</u> of the bricks in the box." "Find the picture with <u>none</u> of the bricks in the box."
"Find the picture with <u>all</u> of the bricks in the box."

"Tell me which objects are blue." "Tell me which objects are brown." "Tell me which objects are green."

Side 1 _____

Lesson 135   Name _____

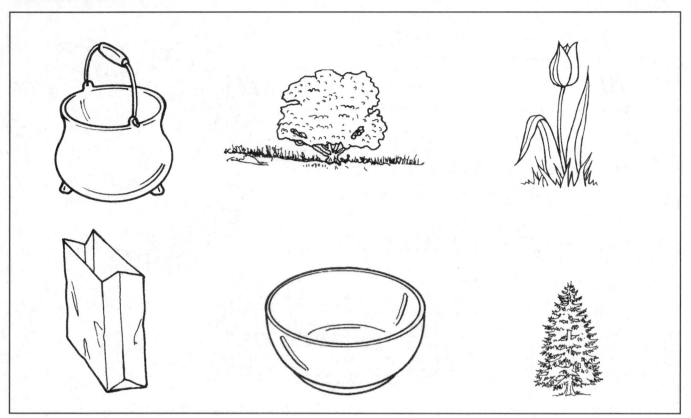

"What kind of objects did you draw triangles around?" "What kind of objects did you draw rectangles around?"

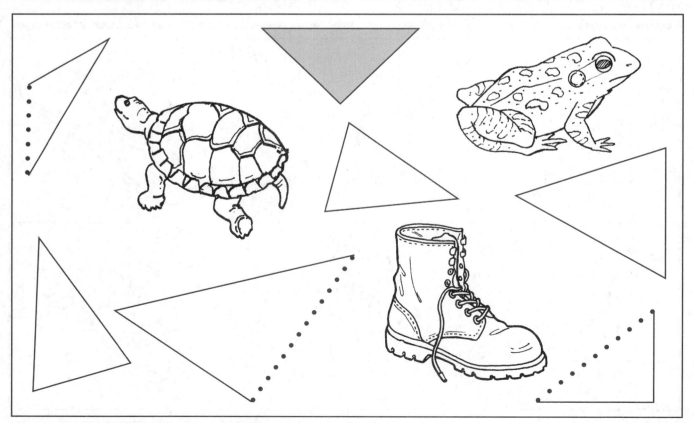

"Show me the triangles that you finished." "What color are they?"

Side 2 _____

Lesson 136   Name _____

"What kind of objects did you circle?" "What kind of objects did you draw rectangles around?"

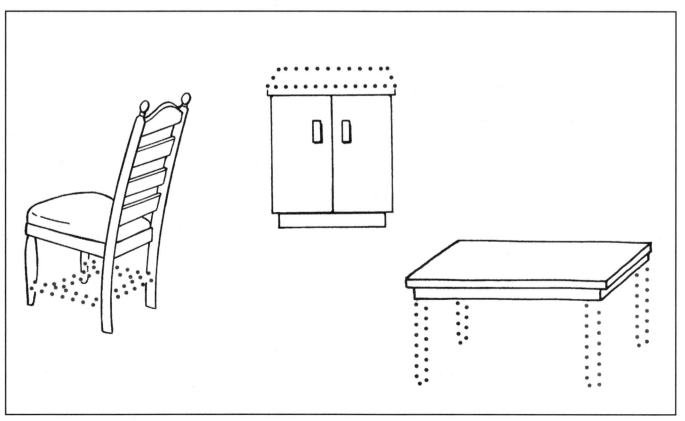

For each object, ask, "What is this?" "Which part was missing?"

Lesson 136   Name _____

"What's in the top two boxes?" "Tell me what you drew to fix the other boxes." "What did you cross out?"

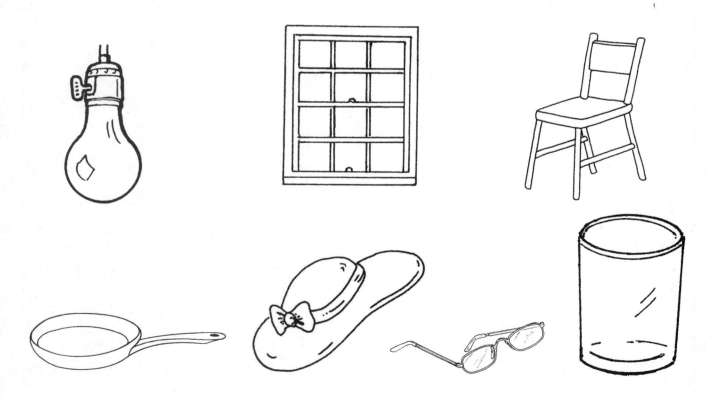

"What kind of objects did you color blue?" "What are the other objects?"

Side 2 _____

Lesson 137   Name _____

"Are all of the eggs in the basket?" "Are some of the eggs broken?" "Are all of the cats yellow?"

"Is the red duck wet?" "Is the dog with a collar short?"

Side 1 _____

Lesson 137   Name _____

"Show me the rectangles that you finished." "What color are they?"

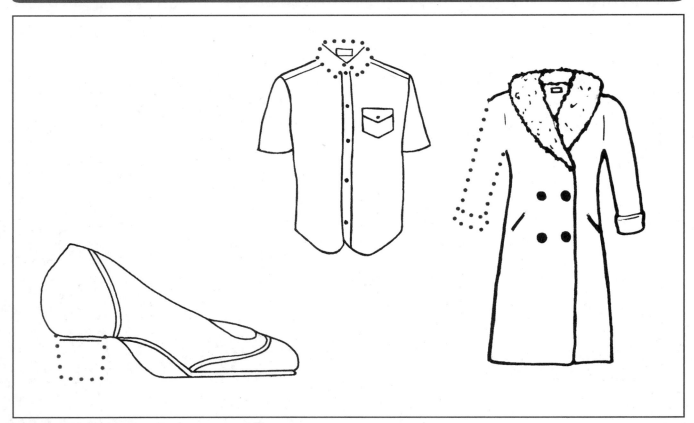

For each object, ask, "What is this?" "Which part was missing?"

Side 2 _____

Lesson 138   Name _____

"Is the object that's crossed out cold?" "Is the object with ice in it full?"

"Find the picture with <u>all</u> of the cars in the street." "Find the picture with <u>some</u> of the cars in the street." "Find the picture with <u>none</u> of the cars in the street."

Side 1 _____

Lesson 138   Name _____

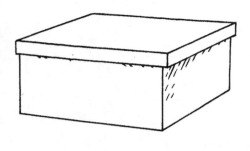  

  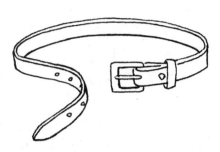

"What kind of objects are brown?" "What are the other objects?"

"What place is in the picture?" "What did you color black?" "What did you color brown?" "What did you color blue?"

Side 2 _____

Lesson 139   Name _____

"Are some of the kittens black?" "Are they in the box?" "Are all of the kittens brown?" "Are they next to the box?" "Are all of the puppies black?"

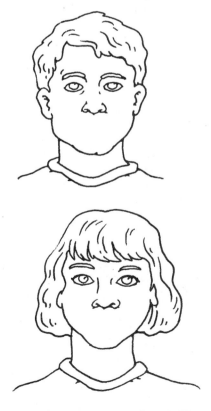

"Are the men sad?" "Are the women happy?"

Side 1 _____

Lesson 139   Name _____

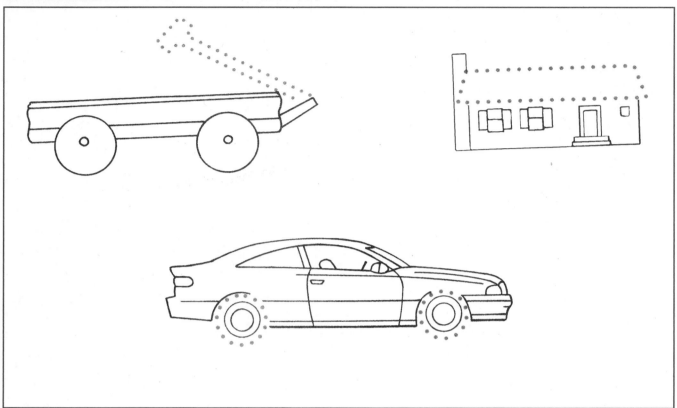

For each object, ask, "What is this?" "Which part was missing?"

"What's in the circle?" "Name the objects that belong in the circle." "Name the ones that don't belong."

Side 2 _____

Lesson 140   Name _____

"Are the big children happy?" "Do the small children have their mouths closed?"

"What kind of objects did you circle?" "What kind of objects did you draw triangles around?" "What are the other objects?"

Side 1 _____

Lesson 140   Name _____

"Which pigs are wearing hats?" "Which animals are brown?" "Which puppies are wearing glasses?"

"What's in the circle?" "Name the objects that belong in the circle." "Name the objects that don't belong."

Side 2 _____

Lesson 141   Name _____

"What color are the containers that are under the table?" "What color are the containers that are on the table?" "What else is in the picture?"

"Find the picture with <u>some</u> of the ducks in the pond." "Find the picture with <u>none</u> of the ducks in the pond." "Find the picture with <u>all</u> of the ducks in the pond."

Lesson 141   Name _____

"Is the black door open?" "Is the broken window closed?"

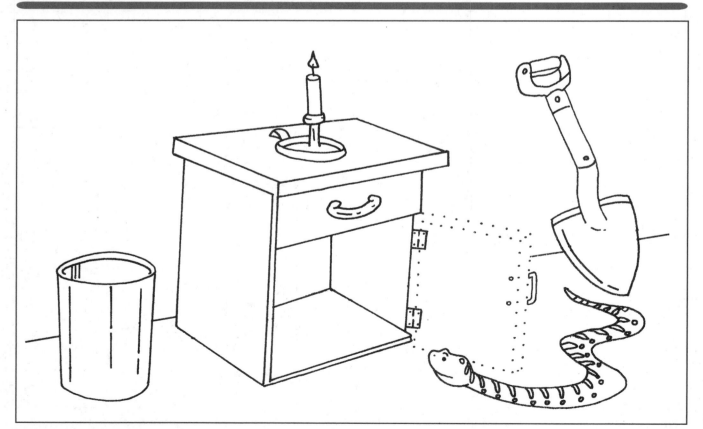

"Tell me the parts of the cabinet." "Which part was missing?"

Side 2 _____

Lesson 142   Name _____

"Are any of the black animals small?" "Is the brown animal fast?" "Are the slow animals wearing hats?"

"Tell me the parts of the wagon." "Which part was missing?"

Side 1 _____

Lesson 142   Name _____

"What's in the circle?" "Name the objects that belong in the circle." "Name the objects that don't belong."

"What's the same about the connected objects in the first box?" "What did you cross out?" Repeat for second and third boxes.

Side 2 _____

Lesson 143   Name _____

"Are the wet boys sad?" "Are the dry boys happy?"

For each object, ask, "What is this?" "What part was missing?"

Side 1 _____

Lesson 143   Name _____

"What kind of objects did you color green?" "What kind of objects did you circle?"

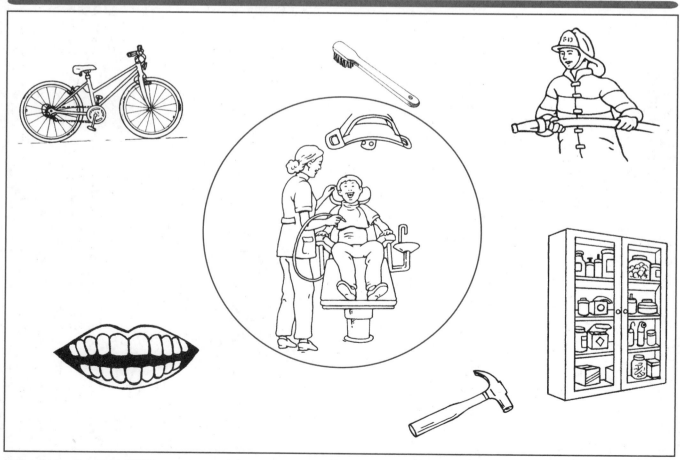

"What's in the circle?" "Name the objects that belong in the circle." "Name the objects that don't belong."

Side 2 _____

Lesson 144   Name _____

"Show me the circles that you finished." "What color are they?"

"What's in the top two boxes?" "Tell me what you drew to fix the other boxes." "What did you cross out?"

Side 1 _____

Lesson 144   Name _____

"What's in the circle?" "Name the objects that belong in the circle." "Name the ones that don't belong."

 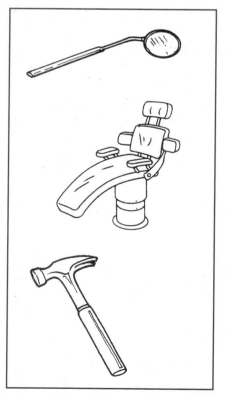 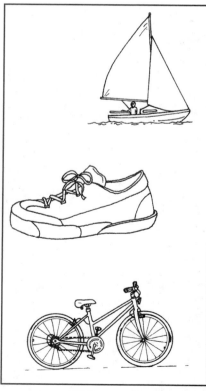

"What's the same about the connected objects in the first box?" "What did you cross out?" Repeat for second and third boxes.

Side 2 _____

Lesson 145   Name _____

"Tell me the parts of the coat." "Which part was missing?"

"What kind of objects are brown?" "What did you cross out?"

Side 1 _____

Lesson 145   Name _____

"What's in the circle?" "Name the objects that belong in the circle." "Name the ones that don't belong."

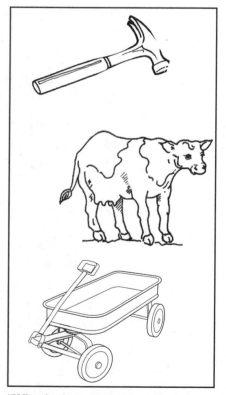

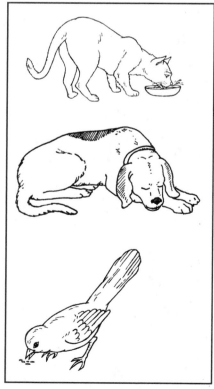

"What's the same about the connected objects in the first box?" "What did you cross out?" Repeat for second and third boxes.

Side 2 _____

Lesson 146　　Name _____

"What kind of objects did you circle?" "What kind of objects did you draw rectangles around?" "What objects are left over?"

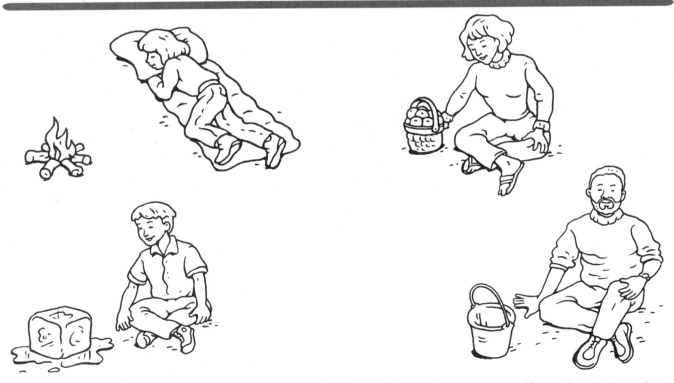

"Is the person wearing green sitting next to something hot?" "Is the person wearing yellow next to a container that's empty?" "Are the people wearing glasses asleep?"

Side 1 _____

Lesson 146   Name _____

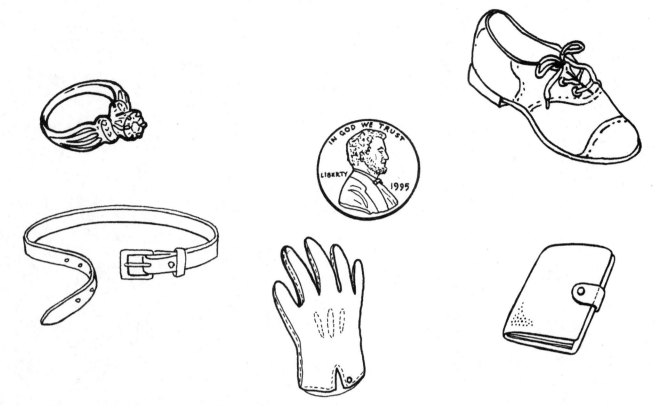

"What kind of objects are brown?" "What kind of objects did you draw triangles around?"

"What's in the circle?" "Name the objects that belong in the circle." "Name the ones that don't belong."

Side 2 _____

Lesson 147   Name _____

"What kind of animals are black?" "What are some of the birds holding?" "What are all of the monkeys wearing?"

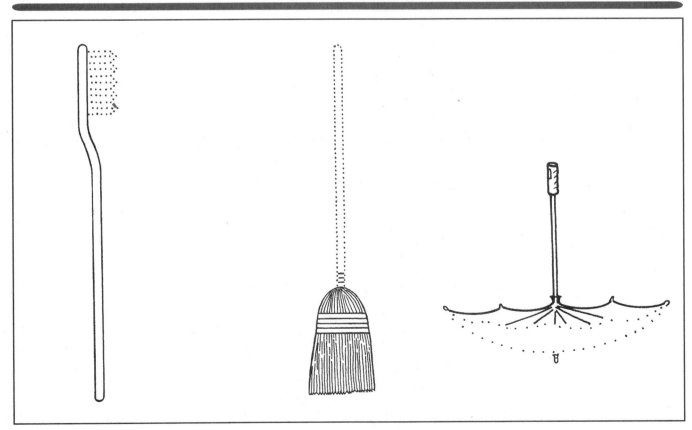

For each object, ask, "What is this?" "Which part was missing?"

Side 1 _____

Lesson 147   Name _____

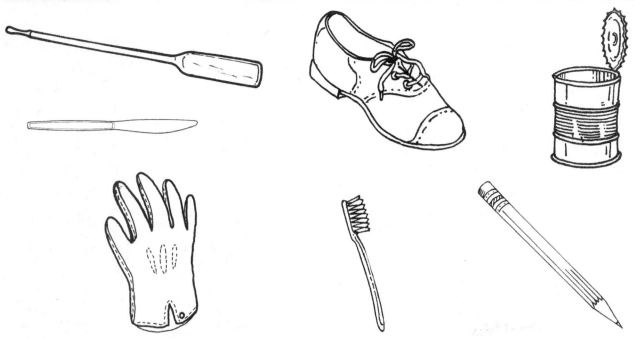

"What kind of objects are red?" "What kind of objects are blue?" "What kind of objects are yellow?"

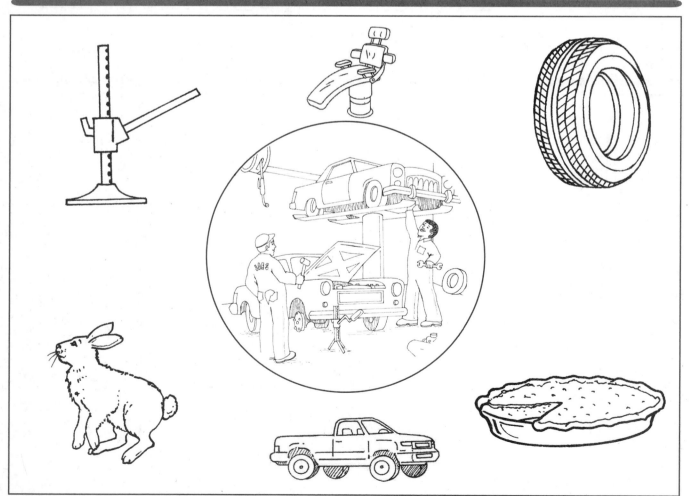

"What's in the circle?" "Name the objects that belong in the circle." "Name the ones that don't belong."

Side 2 _____

Lesson 148   Name _____

"Where do the white animals go?" "Where do the black ones go?"

"What kind of objects did you circle?" "What kind of objects did you draw rectangles around?"

Side 1 _____

Lesson 148   Name _____

"What's in the top two boxes?" "Tell me what you drew to fix the other boxes." "What did you cross out?"

"What's in the circle?" "Name the objects that belong in the circle." "Name the ones that don't belong."

Side 2 _____

Lesson 149   Name _____

"Are all the blue animals in boats?" "Are all the red animals in boats?" "Are some of the animals with long whiskers wet?"

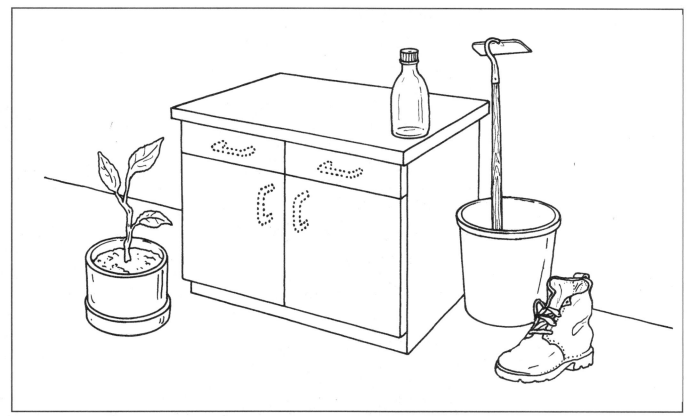

"Tell me the parts of the cabinet." "Which part was missing?"

Side 1 _____

Lesson 149   Name _____

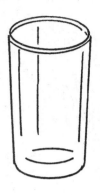

"What kind of objects are brown?" "What kind of objects are green?"

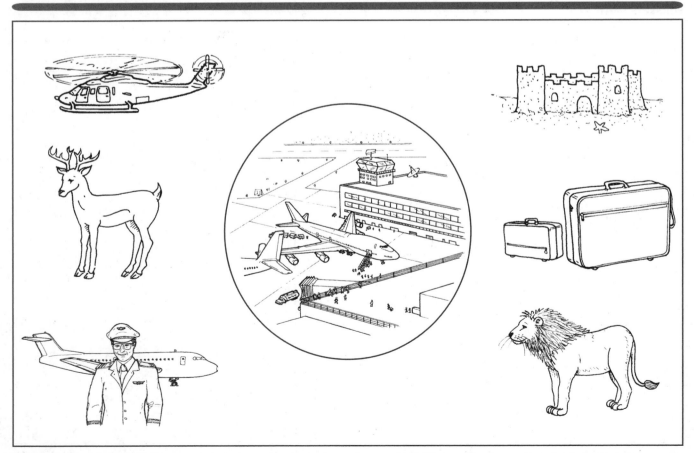

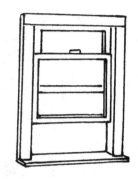

"What's in the circle?" "Name the objects that belong in the circle." "Name the ones that don't belong."

Side 2 _____

Lesson 150　　Name _____

"Tell me which animals go in back of the truck." "Tell me which animals go on top of the truck." "Where do the other animals go?" "What are they?"

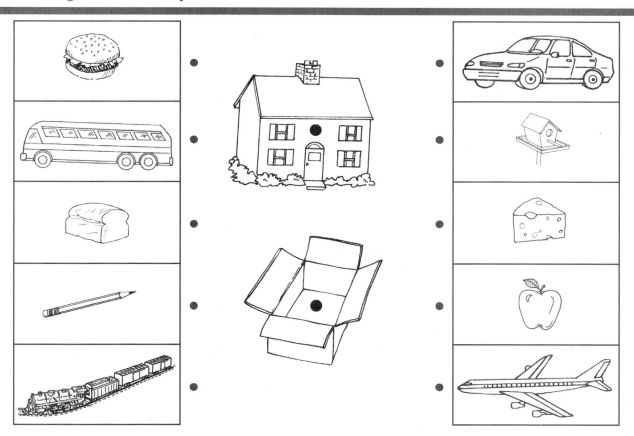

"Are the objects in the building big?" "Are the objects in the container small?"

Side 1 _____

Lesson 150   Name _____

"Is the wet animal small?" "What kind of objects are red?" "Are the black animals big?"

"What's in the top two boxes?" "Tell me what you drew to fix the other boxes." "What did you cross out?"

Side 2 _____